chile aphrodisia

Rio Nuevo Publishers®

P.O. Box 5250, Tucson, Arizona 85703-0250

(520) 623-9558, www.rionuevo.com

Text and photography © 2006 by Rio Nuevo Publishers. Food styling by
Tracy Vega. Many thanks to AJ's Fine Foods and to Jeannine Brookshire for
providing beautiful settings and amenities for the photo shoots for this book.

Photography credits as follows:
W. Ross Humphreys: pages 2-3, 4 (left), 5, 11, 25, 39, 51, 58, 66, front
cover, back cover
Robin Stancliff: pages 4 (right), 19, 37, 45, 49, 63, 71

Library of Congress Cataloging-in-Publication Data
Reiley, Amy.
  Chile aphrodisia / Amy Reiley and Annette Tomei.
    p. cm. — (Cook west series)
  Includes bibliographical references and index.
  ISBN-13: 978-1-887896-90-0 (pbk.)
  ISBN-10: 1-887896-90-2 (pbk.)
  1. Cookery (Hot peppers) I. Tomei, Annette. II. Title. III. Series.
  TX803.P46R45 2006
  641.6'384—dc22

                                2006000386

Shown on this page: Cubanelle peppers. Page 4 (left): Red Fresno chile.
Page 5: Chile de árbol ristras.

Design: Karen Schober, Seattle, Washington.
Printed in Korea.
10 9 8 7 6 5 4 3 2 1

chile
aphrodisia

AMY REILEY and ANNETTE TOME

RIO NUEVO PUBLISHERS
TUCSON, ARIZONA

COOK WEST
SERIES

contents

xxxxxx

It has long been said that chile is good for the soul. But what most philosophers don't realize is that the chile's true ability lies not in enhancing the soul but in increasing libido.

Staples of the naturopathic medicine traditions in both the East and the West, chile peppers have been used to treat conditions from headaches to arthritis, bursitis, and lupus, as well as for pain relief. And the same compound, capsaicin, which makes chiles such potent natural healers, also sets them to work on the libido. Capsaicin, the primary component in giving a chile its "heat," is one of the finest natural ingredients for raising body temperature and increasing blood flow. Biting into a tongue-teasing pepper can mimic, or more ideally, enhance the feelings of romance.

Although the FDA maintains that no food is a proven aphrodisiac to humans, the miracles of modern science have shown that chiles can cause an aphrodisiac reaction—at least in water fleas. The theory, tested in a controlled flea arousal experiment, demonstrated that chiles cause the body to release endorphins, thereby replicating the pleasure surge of pure, animal sex.

In Colombia, the surge of chiles is much sought, but not so much as a condiment as a more hard-core "rush." Cut into cocaine, chiles are used to enhance the drug's impact. But the pepper's potency is far more pleasant—and memorable—without the added rush of Colombian "sugar." However, as with any aspect of the art of arousal, it is important to evolve a sense of personal taste. Before applying the potent pepper to an evening of seduction, familiarize yourself with the multitude of different chiles and their potential effectiveness.

There are more than 200 known varieties of chiles and probably hundreds more undiscovered by all but small pockets of rural inhabitants throughout the American Southwest, Mexico, and Central America. More than half of the popular varieties are indigenous to Mexico and the Southwest, where their use dates back further than recorded time.

Evidence from the seventh century B.C. shows signs that chiles were among the first cultivated foods in the world. Their growth and harvesting in the Sonoran Desert by ancient Native Americans is well documented. But there is also evidence that the

Aztecs used chiles more than 900 years ago. Although much of the Aztecs' wisdom was lost in time, the Anasazi culture's knowledge of native chiles—developed more than 600 years ago—is still applied today. Although this book barely scratches the surface of the varieties and uses for chiles, we've incorporated some of our favorites from the heart of the New World, including:

Anaheim Also called the California green chile, this long, shiny green chile is among the mildest and sweetest of the commonly used varieties.

Ancho A dried poblano chile, the ancho has a smoky sweet flavor. It is among the most popular chiles in Mexico.

Chile de árbol A skinny, red, thin-fleshed chile, the dried árbol brings a sharp, hot pepper essence to any dish it touches. It is commonly used to put the burn in hot sauce.

Chipotle A dried, smoked jalapeño, the chipotle has intense heat. Its smoky flavor infuses any food with which it is prepared.

Habañero A truly beautiful chile, the habañero ripens from green to yellow to brilliant orange. One variety does ripen to red, but it is quite rare. It can be dried, but this is not recommended, as its appeal is in its succulent, juicy flavors rather than its heat.

Jalapeño Picked green and served fresh or pickled, the jalapeño is the most widely available chile in the U.S. Fairly mild on the heat scale, as it ripens to red, the heat intensifies. Ripened and smoked, it becomes the chipotle.

New Mexico A large chile, it is similar in size to an Anaheim but offers more heat.

Pasilla (Negro) The dried pasilla, often called the *chile negro,* offers a sharp bite. A large pepper, almost black in color, it can be used for anything from stuffing to frying whole.

Poblano A large, triangular-shaped chile, the poblano is a sweet, thin-skinned variety with a pleasant heat. Fresh, it is commonly served stuffed; dried, it becomes the ancho.

Serrano A small, fresh chile with smooth skin, the serrano's heat level ranges from hot to absolute fire.

Thai A fresh red chile with an oval shape, its heat level is close to that of the habañero.
For more on chile intensity, please refer to the Scoville heat meter on page 75.

Although chiles vary in size, shape, and level of heat, every chile is packed with more vitamin C than an orange. And even though much of the vitamin C content diminishes as the chile is dried, drying increases its vitamin A content by 100 times.

Vitamin rich though they may be, chiles are also known to be addictive. Chile lovers easily fall in love with the endorphin high of sweet heat, craving more and more increasingly hot flavors. And while constant chile consumption can envelop you in a euphoric cloud, chile's potency is far more exciting when taken in small doses at less regular intervals, when it can send a little shock of heat up the spine and down into the loins.

We offer you a collection of chile recipes that can make your lips swell and taste buds dance at any time of day. Whether you prefer a chile-laced breakfast in bed or the seduction of sweet hot cocktails, we've included something to fan your flames of desire.

SOURCES If you have trouble finding any of the less common varieties at your local grocer, here are several reliable online and mail-order sources for quality chiles, both fresh and dried, as well as powdered.

Ethnic Grocer (shop by country/cuisine for bottled, canned, and dried chiles and accessories), www.ethnicgrocer.com

Los Chileros (whole chiles, chile powders, salsas, and mixes), 888-EAT-CHILE, www.888eatchile.com

Melissa's (fresh and dried chiles as well as other high-quality produce), 800-588-0151, www.melissas.com

Moosewood Hollow (makes pure maple syrup infused with habañero peppers), www.infusedmaple.com

Native Seeds/SEARCH (chile powder, whole chiles, smoked chiles from indigenous seed crops), www.nativeseeds.org

Pecos Valley Spice Co. (whole, dried peppers, Southwestern-style spice blends and rubs, pepper seeds), 800-472-8229, www.pecosvalley.com

Santa Cruz Chili & Spice Co. (growing and selling numerous chile varieties and products for more than 60 years), http://santacruzchili.com

Chile de árbol ristra

"Warm Up" Spinach Salad

xxxxxx

Serves 2

4 strips thick-cut bacon, diced

1 teaspoon finely chopped shallots

1/4 cup balsamic vinegar

1/2 teaspoon Dijon mustard

1 teaspoon pepper jelly or jam (made from jalapeños or chipotles)

1/4 teaspoon chipotle chile powder

1/2 cup canola oil

Salt and pepper

2 cups baby spinach leaves, washed and dried

Salt and pepper

1 medium-size pear, cored and thinly sliced

1/4 cup Spicy Sweet Almonds (see page 21)

1/4 cup crumbled goat cheese (chevre)

2 thin slices sweet red onion (optional)

With its sensory explosion of color and contrasting flavors, this starter is the perfect light bite to warm up a night for two.

To make the salad dressing: brown the bacon in a medium saucepan until crispy, then remove the bacon pieces from the pan to a paper towel to drain. Add the shallots to the bacon fat and sauté until translucent. Reduce heat to low and add the vinegar, mustard, jelly or jam, and chipotle powder. Simmer gently. Whisk in the oil and season to taste with salt and pepper. Adjust the amount of oil and chile to your taste. Keep warm. This dressing can be stored in the refrigerator in an air-tight container for up to 1 week. Heat to a boil before each use for safety purposes. After the first or second use, you may need to add a small amount (1 tablespoon or less) of water to thin to original consistency.

To assemble the salads: in a mixing bowl, toss the spinach leaves with a small amount of salt and freshly ground pepper and approximately 2 tablespoons of the warm dressing (adjust amount to your taste). Arrange several slices of pear on each of two plates; top with the dressed spinach greens. Garnish with crispy bacon pieces, almonds, and cheese; top each serving with a thin slice of sweet red onion, if desired.

Chile-Lime Baked Fries

xxxxxx

Deep-fried food can be devastating to the libido, but baking makes this French-fry variation a "safe" choice in cooking with chiles for seduction.

Preheat oven to 450 degrees F. Peel the potatoes and cut them into 1-inch-thick wedges.

In a medium bowl, coat the potatoes with the oil, salt, and pepper. Spread evenly on a sheet pan and bake for approximately 15 minutes, until golden brown.

While the potatoes are roasting, mix the mayonnaise, lime juice, and chile powder.

Remove the potatoes from the oven and toss with the mayonnaise mixture. Serve immediately.

Serves 4

2 potatoes

1 tablespoon canola oil

$1/4$ teaspoon salt

$1/4$ teaspoon
ground pepper

2 tablespoons mayonnaise

Juice of 1 medium lime

$1/2$ teaspoon chile powder
(your choice of chiles)

Fennel-Apple Slaw

xxxxxx

Serves 4–6

1/2 cup buttermilk

1 tablespoon honey

1 teaspoon grainy mustard

1 teaspoon pasilla chile powder

1/2 teaspoon fresh thyme leaves

Salt and pepper

1 Granny Smith apple, cored and julienned

1 teaspoon lemon juice

2 cups thinly sliced napa cabbage

1 Anaheim chile, seeded and julienned

1 small–medium bulb of fennel, cleaned and julienned

4 scallions, sliced thin (white and green parts)

1 teaspoon salt

1/2 teaspoon freshly ground pepper

Apple, fennel, and honey make for a dish not only packed with nutrients but brimming over with aphrodisiac ingredients. Presented in a lettuce leaf "bowl," this slaw makes a great base for the Chilled Grilled Shrimp (see page 15) or Chicken Skewers with Spicy Peanut Dipping Sauce (see page 43).

To make the dressing, combine the buttermilk, honey, mustard, chile powder, thyme, and salt and pepper in a jar with a snug-fitting lid. Shake well, taste, and re-season as needed.

Toss the julienne strips of apple in the lemon juice. In a large bowl, combine the apple strips with the cabbage, chile, fennel, and scallions. Toss to combine well. Season with salt and pepper. Add half of the dressing and mix well; add more if desired. This slaw should be served within 30 minutes of adding the dressing.

Chilled Grilled Shrimp

XXXXXX

The char of the grill in combination with the chile's sweet sting make for a simple but sophisticated dish. It's a flavor combination we love to present whenever we're looking for a starter that offers complexity and ease. These shrimp are great served as simple hors d'oeuvres or arranged on a salad. They are also great on Thai Firecracker Rice (see page 50).

Combine the oil, zests, juices, pepper, and chile slices in a jar with a snug-fitting lid. Shake well.

Place the shrimp in a gallon-size zip-top bag with half the marinade/dressing. Shake and allow to sit in the refrigerator for at least 30 minutes, or up to 2 hours.

Heat the grill or stove-top grill pan to high. Skewer 3 shrimp on each 12-inch skewer so that they will lie flat on the grill; season with salt and pepper. Brush the grill grates lightly with oil. Grill the shrimp for approximately 2–3 minutes per side or until they turn completely pink. Be careful not to overcook. Remove the shrimp from the skewers into a medium bowl.

Toss the grilled shrimp with the remaining marinade, then cover and chill for at least 30 minutes or up to 2 hours.

2 first-course servings, or 8 hors d'oeuvres servings

¼ cup canola oil

Zest of 1 lemon

Zest of 1 lime

2 tablespoons lime juice

2 tablespoons lemon juice

¼ teaspoon ground black pepper

1 Thai chile, sliced

12 medium shrimp or prawns, peeled and deveined

4 bamboo skewers (12 inches long), soaked in water

Salt and pepper

Southeast Asian Ceviche

xxxxxx

Serves 4

1-inch piece of fresh ginger, peeled and finely diced

2 teaspoons finely diced lemongrass

1 tablespoon fish sauce

Zest of 2 limes

³/₄ cup lime juice

¹/₂ cup coconut milk

1 tablespoon honey

1 pound very fresh skinless white fish (snapper, halibut, cod, mahimahi) or scallops, sliced thin

1 mango, peeled and cut into julienne strips

1 Thai chile, seeds and ribs removed, finely sliced

¹/₂ red bell pepper, seeds and ribs removed, cut into julienne strips

¹/₂ cup finely sliced scallions

Salt and pepper

¹/₄ cup chopped cilantro leaves for garnish

Although ceviche is a Latin American dish, the flavors in this recipe are distinctly Asian.

Combine the ginger, lemongrass, fish sauce, lime zest, lime juice, coconut milk, and honey in a blender or food processor. Blend well.

In a non-reactive bowl, combine the fish, mango, chile, bell pepper, and scallions; pour the coconut-lime mixture over and stir until the fish is well coated. Season with salt and pepper to taste. Cover and refrigerate for at least 2 hours or until the fish is "cooked" by the citrus juice.

Serve garnished with the cilantro leaves.

Chile-Citrus Olives

xxxxxx

Olives are salty, pungent, and ever-so-slightly sweet. Few flavors can effectively augment olives' strong notes, but chiles marry beautifully with the Mediterranean fruit.

With a vegetable peeler, remove the top layer of zest from the orange and lemon. Cut the zest into julienne strips. Cut the fruit in half, reserving the juice of half the orange and half the lemon.

Heat the olive oil over medium heat in a sauté pan; add the chiles, zest, and garlic. Sauté for 2 minutes to release the essential oils.

In a non-reactive bowl, toss the olives with the warm oil mixture, along with the juices and harissa sauce. Cover and refrigerate for at least 2 hours. Good for at least 1 month if stored in the refrigerator.

Makes approximately 2 cups

1 medium orange

1 lemon

1/2 cup extra-virgin olive oil

2 chiles de árbol

2 cloves garlic, cut in half lengthwise

2 cups cracked green olives (or good-quality olives of your choice), drained

2 teaspoons Spicy Onion Harissa (see page 55)

Brie Apple Quesadillas

xxxxxx

*2 regular servings, or
appetizers for 4*

1 large Granny Smith apple
1 New Mexico red chile
4 ounces Brie cheese
4 flour tortillas (10-inch size)
2 tablespoons butter

Perhaps more Normandy than New Mexico, this simple small bite fuses flavors from across the pond with traditional, Southwestern heat.

Core and quarter the apple; slice thinly. Remove the seeds and ribs from the chile; cut into julienne strips.

Cut the Brie into an even number of thin slices.

Spread the Brie evenly over each of two tortillas. Arrange the apple slices evenly in a single layer over the Brie and top evenly with the julienne strips of red chile. Cover each with the remaining tortillas.

Heat a griddle or large sauté pan. Spread butter on both sides of each quesadilla. Cook each quesadilla for approximately 3 minutes per side, until light gold in color and the cheese melts. Cut each quesadilla into quarters or eighths. Serve with a green salad garnished with spiced pecans, or offer as casual hors d'ouevres.

Chile Corn Chowder

xxxxxx

4 servings

1 poblano chile

2 ears of corn, shucked and cleaned

2 cups milk

2 teaspoons light oil

4 pieces of thick-sliced bacon, diced

½ cup diced onion

1 rib of celery, diced

1 russet potato, peeled and diced small

2 cups chicken or vegetable stock

Zest of 1 lime

¼ cup finely diced red bell pepper

1 tablespoon fresh lime juice

Salt and pepper

Tabasco sauce

Grated pepper Jack cheese, for garnish

Thinly sliced scallion tops (green parts), for garnish

Soups and stews are perfect dishes for showcasing chiles, where their heat can kiss the dish's every inch. But what makes a chile-infused chowder work is the more subtle ingredients—in this case, sweet corn and milk—that serve as a foil for the chile's potential sting.

Roast the chile over the open flame of a stove burner until charred on all sides. Place in a brown paper bag or covered bowl to cool. When the chile is cool, rub off the charred skin, remove the seeds and ribs, and dice fine.

Cut corn kernels from the cob and set aside. Break the cobs in half, place them in a 1½-quart saucepan with the milk, and bring to a simmer over medium heat. Do not scald the milk. After it comes to a simmer, remove the milk from the heat and allow to steep for 30 minutes. Strain, discarding all the solids.

In a stockpot, heat the oil. Add the bacon and cook until crisp. Remove the bacon and allow it to drain on a plate covered with a paper towel. Add the onion to the bacon fat, sautéing until tender. Add the celery and potato; sauté for 2 minutes. Add the stock; bring to a boil over medium-high heat. Reduce heat and simmer until potatoes are cooked through.

Add the milk infusion, corn kernels, bacon, lime zest, diced poblano, and diced red pepper. Simmer until heated through. Add the lime juice, then season to taste with salt, pepper, and Tabasco sauce. Serve hot, garnished with a sprinkling of grated pepper Jack cheese and thinly sliced scallion greens.

Spicy Sweet Almonds

xxxxxx

An easy make-ahead hors d'oeuvre, this recipe perfectly fits the bill when you're looking for a pairing with sweet, tangy drinks, such as a summer agua fresca or fresh-made mojito. Amy thinks it tastes even better on an autumn afternoon, served in her hammock built for two.

Preheat oven to 325 degrees F. Combine sugar and water in a small saucepan. Bring to a boil for 1 minute. Remove from heat and stir in the almonds. Allow to sit for 2 minutes.

Combine the salt, chile powder, and dry mustard in a mixing bowl. Drain the almonds and toss them in with the spices, then drizzle with butter. Spread on a baking sheet in a single layer.

Bake for 7–10 minutes. Cool thoroughly before serving.

Makes approximately 1 cup

1/4 cup sugar

1/4 cup water

1 cup raw almonds

1 teaspoon salt

1/2 teaspoon red chile powder

1/4 teaspoon dry mustard

1 tablespoon butter, melted

South American Ceviche

xxxxxx

Serves 4

12 medium-large raw shrimp, peeled and deveined, cut into bite-size pieces

2 Roma tomatoes, seeded and diced

1 green jalapeño, seeds and ribs removed, finely diced

1 red jalapeño, seeds and ribs removed, finely diced

1/2 cup chopped scallions

Zest of 2 lemons

Zest of 2 limes

Zest of 2 oranges

1/2 cup lemon juice

1/2 cup lime juice

1/2 cup orange juice

1 teaspoon honey

Hot sauce, such as Tabasco or Frank's Red Hot

Salt and pepper, to taste

This recipe is an adaptation of a traditional Ecuadorian dish. The flavors and ingredients are native to the Americas, and its sneaky heat will please the tongue and warm the soul.

Combine all ingredients in a non-reactive bowl. Stir well. Cover and refrigerate for at least 2 hours or until the shrimp is "cooked" by the citrus juice.

Sicilian-Style Stuffed Peppers

xxxxxx

Though they are a member of the Capiscum family, the sweet peppers used in this recipe are low enough on the Scoville scale (categorized with bell peppers) that they may not be considered true "chiles." What can we say? We have a weakness for a perfectly stuffed pepper.

Serves 4

Preheat oven to 375 degrees F. Place chopped raisins in a small microwave-safe bowl; fill with enough water to cover the raisins. Cover the bowl and microwave for 1 minute. Allow to cool. Make slits lengthwise from stem to tip on each pepper. Remove the seeds while maintaining the pepper's shape.

In a medium sauté pan, heat the olive oil over medium-high heat. Add the anchovies, breaking them up in the oil with a wooden spoon and allowing them to melt into the oil. Add the onion and sauté until tender. Add the loose Italian sausage, browning well and breaking up with the wooden spoon. Add the raisins, bread crumbs, and piñon nuts; sauté for 2–3 minutes, stirring often. Remove from the heat.

Stir the grated Parmesan cheese, basil, and tomato puree into the stuffing mixture. Season with salt and pepper. Divide the mixture evenly, stuffing each pepper.

Set stuffed peppers in a 13 x 9 x 2-inch baking pan with approximately ¼ inch of warm water and a tablespoon of olive oil. Top with grated provolone cheese. Bake for approximately 30 minutes or until peppers are tender and the cheese is melted and light golden in color.

Ingredients:

- 2 tablespoons golden raisins, chopped
- 4 sweet Italian frying peppers (cubanelles or banana peppers)
- 1 tablespoon olive oil
- 2 anchovy fillets
- ¼ cup finely diced onion
- 2 hot Italian sausages (about 8 ounces), casings removed
- ½ cup dry bread crumbs
- 2 tablespoons toasted piñon nuts
- 1 cup grated Parmesan cheese
- 1 tablespoon freshly chopped basil
- ¼ cup tomato puree
- Salt and pepper
- 1 tablespoon olive oil
- ½ cup grated provolone cheese

White Gazpacho

xxxxxx

Serves 4–6

2 cups green seedless grapes, cut in half

1/2 English cucumber, peeled, seeded, and cut into chunks

1/2 cup slivered, blanched almonds

2 tablespoons chopped scallions (white and light green parts only)

1 jalapeño, seeds and ribs removed, chopped

2 tablespoons sherry vinegar

2 tablespoons almond oil (can be replaced with canola oil)

2 teaspoons honey

1/2 cup whipping cream

Salt and pepper

Toasted almond slices, for garnish

Chopped chives, for garnish

What do you get when you cross ancient Greece with the Southwest? A perfectly piquant dish with sensually stimulating texture and taste. Enjoy this chilled soup alone or with a crisp green salad.

In a blender, puree the grapes, cucumber, almonds, scallions, jalapeño, vinegar, oil, and honey. With the blender running, slowly add the cream. Season to taste.

Chill thoroughly before serving. Garnish with toasted almond slices and chopped chives.

Pasilla chile.

"Good Morning, Hottie!" Cakes

xxxxxx

Makes 10–12 pancakes

¹/₄ cup chopped
dried cherries

2 tablespoons
cranberry juice

¹/₂ cup cornmeal

¹/₂ cup milk, warmed

¹/₂ cup all-purpose flour

1 teaspoon baking soda

1¹/₂ teaspoons
baking powder

2 tablespoons sugar

¹/₂ teaspoon salt

1 teaspoon ancho
chile powder

3 tablespoons
butter, melted

2 eggs

¹/₂ teaspoon vanilla extract

1 cup maple syrup

1 teaspoon ancho
chile powder

It is utter bliss to wake up to a plate of steaming hottie cakes. A tongue tease of sweet and heat, these cakes have a way of making breakfast last all day.

Place chopped cherries and cranberry juice in a microwave-safe bowl. Cover and heat on high for 1 minute to rehydrate the cherries. Set aside to cool. Preheat the oven to 250 degrees F.

In a medium-large mixing bowl, combine cornmeal and warm milk. Allow to sit for 5 minutes. In another bowl, combine flour, baking soda, baking powder, sugar, salt, and chile powder.

Stir the melted butter into the cornmeal mixture. Add the eggs and vanilla, stirring until well combined.

Whisk in the dry ingredients until all are moist. Add the cherries and any remaining liquid. Allow to sit for 3–5 minutes. Meanwhile, in a small saucepan, combine the maple syrup and second teaspoon of chile powder. Bring to a simmer and keep warm until served.

To cook the pancakes, heat a non-stick skillet over medium-high heat. Spray with cooking spray. Using a 2-ounce ladle or ¼-cup measuring cup, pour the batter into the pan, allowing space between each pancake. Cook until edges are dry and bubbles form in the center (approximately 2–3 minutes). Flip pancakes and cook for another minute. Cook in batches, holding the finished cakes on an oven-safe plate or cookie sheet in the oven.

Serve the pancakes immediately with the warm syrup and butter.

Variations The ancho chile powder gives the pancakes a smoky, earthy flavor with only a hint of heat. For spicier pancakes and/or syrup, use chipotle powder or hot New Mexico chile powder instead of ancho powder. Instead of making your own chile syrup, you may wish to try "Sweet Heat" maple syrup infused with habañero peppers from Moosewood Hollow (see page 10).

French Toast "Rellenos"

xxxxxx

Serves 2–4

4 ounces cream cheese

1/2 cup grated
Cheddar cheese

2 Anaheim chiles, roasted,
peeled, and diced

2 scallions, thinly
sliced (whites and part
of the greens)

1/2 teaspoon salt

1/4 teaspoon ground black
pepper

Tabasco or other
favorite bottled hot sauce

2 eggs

1/2 cup half-and-half

Salt and pepper

1/4 teaspoon hot
chile powder

4 slices of good French,
Italian, or Brioche-style
bread (1 inch thick)

Cooking spray or canola
oil for the griddle

A savory French toast reminiscent of chiles rellenos, this unique extravagance dresses up an American classic with Southwestern flavor.

To prepare the filling: In a medium mixing bowl, cream the cream cheese and Cheddar together. Add the chiles, scallions, salt, pepper, and hot sauce; mix well.

In another medium mixing bowl, scramble together the eggs and half-and-half; season with salt, pepper, and chile powder. Heat a griddle or large sauté pan over medium-high heat. Heat oven to 200 degrees F.

Make a horizontal cut into each piece of bread, creating a pocket (do not cut all the way through). Fill each slice of bread evenly with the chile-cheese mixture. Spray or oil the griddle. Soak each piece with the egg batter and transfer to the griddle immediately. Cook until golden brown on both sides and the filling is warm, approximately 3 minutes per side. Transfer to the oven to keep warm while you cook the remaining pieces. Serve hot with a chile-infused maple syrup (see "Good Morning, Hottie!" Cakes recipe on page 26), with your favorite salsa, or with butter and a dusting of powdered sugar.

Green Chile Eggs Benny

xxxxxx

Bringing a Southwestern twist to Sunday brunch, here is a crowd pleaser for family gatherings as well as the perfect private celebration meal for an intimate weekend for two.

In a medium saucepan, combine the beans, scallions, jalapeño, tomato, and lime juice. Heat over medium-high heat; simmer for 5 minutes until the beans are heated through. Season with salt and pepper. Reduce heat and keep warm.

In a medium mixing bowl, combine the *crema* (or crème fraîche), diced roasted poblanos, lime zest, and chile powder. Season with salt and pepper. Allow to sit for 10 minutes or longer before serving.

Poach the eggs and toast the English muffins. On each of 4 plates, lay 2 English muffin halves topped with a slice of ham (optional). Ladle 2–3 tablespoons of black bean mixture over each muffin half. Gently place a poached egg over the beans. Spoon 1 tablespoon of the *crema* mixture over each egg, and garnish with chopped chives and a lime wedge.

Serves 4

1 can (14 ounces) low-sodium black beans, drained and rinsed

2 scallions, sliced thin (white and green parts)

1 jalapeño, seeds and ribs removed, diced

1 tomato, seeded and diced

1 tablespoon lime juice

Salt and pepper

1 cup Mexican crema or crème fraîche

2 poblano chiles, roasted, peeled, seeds and stems removed, diced

Zest of one lime

1 teaspoon New Mexico red chile powder

Salt and pepper

8 large eggs, poached

4 English muffins, toasted

8 slices of ham, optional

2 tablespoons chopped chives, for garnish

4 lime wedges, for garnish

Carne Asada Sandwiches

xxxxxx

2 servings

2 tablespoons canola oil

1 tablespoon lime juice (or other fruit juice)

1 chile de árbol, split

1/4 teaspoon ground black pepper

1 clove garlic, roughly chopped

1/2 pound chuck, sirloin, or round steak

2 tablespoons mayonnaise

Zest of 1 lime

Tabasco or other favorite bottled hot sauce

1 large red bell pepper

1 poblano chile

2 thick slices red onion

1 tablespoon olive oil

Salt and pepper

2 squares focaccia (5 inches each), or other hearty sandwich bread or roll, split

1 ripe avocado, peeled, pitted, and sliced

You will never look at lunchtime in the same way after experiencing one of these over-the-top indulgent sandwiches.

Mix the canola oil, lime juice, chile de árbol, ground black pepper, and garlic with the beef in a gallon-size zip-top bag. Place the bag in a bowl in the refrigerator, and allow the meat to marinate for 1 to 24 hours.

Heat a grill or stove-top grill pan to high. Make the sandwich spread: mix the mayonnaise with the lime zest and hot sauce, to taste. Roast the red bell pepper and the poblano over open flame until the skin is blackened. Place them in a brown paper bag or covered bowl to cool. When cool to the touch, rub off all charred skin, remove stems and seeds, and cut into 1-inch-wide strips.

Drizzle the onion slices with the olive oil, season with salt and pepper, then place on grill for 4 minutes per side. Remove the steak from the marinade; discard the marinade. Season the steak with salt and pepper, then grill for approximately 3–5 minutes per side, to the desired degree of doneness. Allow the steak to rest for 10 minutes before slicing thinly on the bias.

Assemble the sandwiches on the focaccia with the spread, sliced steak, roasted pepper and chile, grilled onion, and avocado slices, as desired.

Chile Mac 'n' Cheese

xxxxxx

A favorite comfort food, spiced up for a warm, cozy fireside snuggle.

4 servings

6 ounces dry rotelle pasta (corkscrew shape)

1 tablespoon butter

2 teaspoons all-purpose flour

1 cup milk (not skim), at room temperature

3/4 cup grated sharp Cheddar cheese

3/4 cup grated pepper Jack cheese

1/2 cup diced poblano chiles

Pinch of nutmeg

Salt and pepper

Cooking spray

1/2 cup grated pepper Jack cheese

Preheat oven to 300 degrees F. Cook pasta as directed on the package, reducing the cooking time so pasta is not quite done. Drain pasta and cool by running cold water over it. Drain well. Pour pasta into a large mixing bowl.

In a 1-quart saucepan, melt butter over medium-high heat. Sprinkle flour over the melted butter, stirring well with a wooden spoon until no lumps remain. Add 1/4 cup of the milk and stir until smooth.

Whisk in the remaining milk slowly, to prevent lumps from forming. Reduce the heat to low; simmer, whisking constantly until the sauce begins to thicken.

Add Cheddar, the 3/4 cup of pepper Jack cheese, and diced chiles, stirring with the wooden spoon until the cheese is melted; do not allow the sauce to boil after adding the cheese. Season with nutmeg, salt, and pepper.

Pour the cheese sauce over the pasta and stir well to coat. Pour the mixture into an 8-inch baking dish coated with cooking spray, then spread the remaining 1/2 cup of pepper Jack cheese evenly over the top.

Bake for 30 minutes or until golden brown. Allow to cool for 5–10 minutes before serving.

Skiers' Chili

xxxxxx

6–8 hearty servings

1 pound dry Great Northern beans, soaked overnight in water, rinsed well

1 quart chicken stock

2 cloves garlic, chopped

1 cup diced onion

1 tablespoon Mexican oregano

1 tablespoon ground cumin

1 tablespoon ground coriander

$1/2$ teaspoon ground cloves

1 bay leaf

6 strips thick-sliced bacon, diced

4 boneless, skinless chicken breasts, diced

Salt and pepper

1 cup diced New Mexico green chiles

2 cups chicken stock

A throwback to Annette's days on the slopes in Utah, this dish was her trick for warming up to an evening of romance. This chili is great served with an assortment of colorful garnishes. Try chopped cilantro, diced red onion, grated pepper Jack and/or Cheddar cheese, sour cream, diced fresh tomatoes, sliced black olives, and a side of warm corn or flour tortillas.

In a stockpot, combine the presoaked beans, 1 quart of chicken stock, garlic, onion, oregano, cumin, coriander, cloves, and bay leaf. Heat to a simmer over high heat, stirring occasionally. Reduce the heat and hold at a simmer for approximately 1½ hours until beans are almost tender. Stir and skim the surface occasionally.

In a sauté pan, cook the diced bacon until crisp. Remove from the pan and drain on a plate covered with a paper towel. In the same pan, brown the diced chicken in the bacon fat, cooking for approximately 5 minutes until chicken is cooked through, then season the chicken with salt and pepper.

Add the chicken, bacon, chiles, and 2 cups of chicken stock to the beans and allow to simmer for an additional hour. Season well with salt and pepper.

Cuban-Style Roast Pork

xxxxxx

The Cubans truly understand the potential for transforming a basic cut of meat into undeniably sensual cuisine.

To prepare the rub, in either a food processor or mortar and pestle, grind the garlic, chile, and oregano into a paste. Rub the roast with the garlic paste, then season with salt and pepper. Place the roast, the juices, and the sherry in a gallon-size zip-top storage bag in a bowl in the refrigerator for at least 2 hours, or overnight if possible. Turn twice to marinate evenly.

Preheat the oven to 350 degrees F. In a non-reactive bowl, toss the onion rings with salt and allow to sit for 10 minutes. Drain the onions and toss with the olive oil. Spray a roasting pan with cooking spray, then line the pan with the onions. Remove the roast from the marinade, patting it dry with paper towels (reserve the marinade). Place the roast on top of the onions.

Roast the pork uncovered for 1 hour. Pour the reserved marinade over the pork and onions and continue cooking, basting frequently with the pan juices, for another hour.

When the roast reaches an internal temperature of 165 degrees F, remove it from the oven; move the roast to a carving board and cover with aluminum foil. Allow it to rest for 15 minutes. Meanwhile, strain the pan juices into a saucepan, reserving the onions. Bring the juices to a simmer, then skim off excess fat. Season to taste and return the onions to the sauce.

Slice the pork; serve with the onion sauce over rice.

Serves 6–8

4 cloves garlic, crushed

1 serrano chile, chopped

1/2 teaspoon Mexican oregano

3–4 pounds boneless pork loin (ask your butcher to trim and tie it into a roast)

Salt and pepper

1/4 cup lime juice

1/4 cup orange juice

1 cup dry sherry

2 large red onions, peeled and cut into thick rings

1/2 teaspoon salt

1 tablespoon olive oil

Cooking spray

Cooked rice

Grilled Pork Chops with Sweet-Hot Roasted Root Vegetables

xxxxxx

4 servings

1 quart water

$1/4$ cup brown sugar

2 tablespoons kosher salt

1 tablespoon black peppercorns

2 cloves garlic

1 habañero chile, split

4 pork loin chops, 1 inch thick

1 medium-size yam, peeled and diced

1 small bulb of fennel, cleaned and diced

2 medium Yukon Gold potatoes, diced

4 cipollini onions, peeled and halved

1 apple, cored and diced

1 large red beet, peeled and diced

$1/2$ habañero chile, seeds and ribs very carefully removed, diced fine

2 teaspoons salt

1 teaspoon fresh ground pepper

$1/4$ cup olive oil

2 tablespoons balsamic vinegar

$1/4$ cup maple syrup

Salt and pepper

The pork chops should be brined one day in advance, if possible. Although it takes a little extra prep and advance planning, your work will pay off in tasting experience.

To make the brine, combine the water, brown sugar, kosher salt, peppercorns, garlic, and chile in a saucepan. Heat until the sugar is dissolved, then cool the mixture completely. To brine the pork, place it in a gallon-size zip-top plastic bag with the brine. Place the bag in a bowl in the refrigerator for 24 hours (turn twice during that time).

Preheat the grill or, if you prefer to prepare the vegetables in the oven, preheat it to 375 degrees F.

Combine the yam, fennel, potatoes, onions, apple, beet, chile half, salt, pepper, olive oil, vinegar, and maple syrup in a large bowl, tossing well to coat evenly. To cook on the grill, make a double-layer pouch from heavy-duty foil by placing the vegetables in the center and folding the edges carefully to prevent leaking. Transfer the pouch to the grill on a baking sheet. Allow approximately 1 hour for the vegetables to cook on the grill. If you prefer to bake them in the oven, prepare a 13 x 9 x 2-inch baking pan with cooking spray, add the vegetables, and cover with foil. Roast for approximately 45 minutes or until vegetables are tender. Season with salt and pepper as necessary before serving.

Remove the pork from the brine and pat dry with paper towels. Discard the brine. Season with salt and pepper. Grill over hot coals for approximately 8–10 minutes per side or until they reach 155 degrees F. The pork chops can also be prepared in the oven on a foil-covered baking sheet for approximately 20 minutes, or until 155 degrees F. Allow the meat to rest for 10 minutes before serving.

Mediterranean Crusted Halibut

xxxxxx

4 servings

3/4 cup fine bread crumbs

1 tablespoon
capers, chopped

3 oil-packed sun-dried
tomatoes, chopped fine

1/2 red serrano, jalapeño
or New Mexico chile, seeds
and ribs removed, diced fine

1 tablespoon
chopped fresh basil

2 cloves garlic, chopped fine

2 tablespoons extra-virgin
olive oil

1/4 teaspoon salt

1/4 teaspoon freshly ground
black pepper

Cooking spray

4 halibut fillets,
6 ounces each

Olive oil for brushing

Salt and pepper

While this dish may mingle a few flavors not typically found in a New Mexican kitchen, it is the native heat that brings dimension to the tastes of the Riviera. This is great served on a bed of mashed potatoes with a sauce of Sweet 100 tomatoes that have been halved and heated in extra-virgin olive oil. It is also wonderful served on a bed of arugula that has been lightly dressed with lemon juice, extra-virgin olive oil, salt, and pepper.

To prepare the crust, mix together the bread crumbs, capers, sun-dried tomatoes, chile, basil, garlic, olive oil, salt, and pepper. The consistency should be moist enough to stay together, but not like paste. The crust can be made several days in advance and stored in the refrigerator. It can also be made ahead and frozen in a freezer bag, with all the air pressed out, for up to 2 weeks.

Preheat the oven to 375 degrees F. Prepare a sheet pan with cooking spray. Arrange the halibut fillets on the pan; brush them with olive oil and season with salt and pepper.

Press 3–4 tablespoons of the crust mixture onto the top side of each fillet, forming an even surface approximately ½ inch thick.

Bake for approximately 20 minutes or until fish is cooked through.

Raspberry-Roasted Salmon with Pearl Couscous

xxxxx

4 servings

2 tablespoons canola oil

1/4 cup finely diced onion

1 cup pearl couscous

2 cups chicken stock or water

6 dried apricots, finely diced

2 tablespoons finely diced dried cranberries or cherries

1/4 teaspoon ground cinnamon

1/4 teaspoon red chile flakes

1 teaspoon salt

1/4 teaspoon freshly ground black pepper

Cooking spray

4 fillets wild salmon, 6 ounces each, pin bones removed

Olive oil for brushing

Salt and pepper

1/3 cup Raspberry Glaze (see page 57)

Pearl couscous, also referred to as Israeli couscous, is much larger than standard couscous, resembling tapioca pearls. A light, slightly nutty grain, it is an excellent foil to the sting of red chiles.

Preheat the oven to 350 degrees F.

Heat the oil in a 2-quart saucepan; sauté the onion over medium-high heat until tender. Add the couscous, stirring well and toasting it for 2 minutes. Add the stock (or water), apricots, cranberries or cherries, cinnamon, chile flakes, salt, and pepper; bring to a boil. Reduce heat, cover, and cook for approximately 20 minutes, stirring once or twice. Remove from heat when tender and liquid is absorbed. Season to taste. Fluff with a fork before serving.

While the couscous is cooking, cover a baking sheet with aluminum foil and spray with cooking spray. Arrange the salmon fillets on the baking pan, brush them with olive oil, and season with salt and pepper.

Bake the salmon for 5 minutes. Brush generously with the raspberry glaze, then return them to the oven and bake for another 10 minutes. Brush with raspberry glaze again, then bake for an additional 5 minutes. Check for doneness. The salmon should be flaky and opaque but not overcooked.

Serve the salmon over a bed of the couscous with a green salad or braised greens.

East Meets Southwest

xxxxxx

Red Fresno chile.

"A Kiss to Make it Better" Soup

xxxxxx

Serves 2

2 cups chicken stock

1 tablespoon
finely diced ginger

1/4 serrano chile,
thinly sliced

1 teaspoon finely
sliced lemongrass
(only the tender bulb)

1 teaspoon chopped
cilantro leaves

Salt to taste

No matter the culture, chicken soup has been a home cure for ages. In Asia, ginger and chiles have both been believed to possess medicinal as well as aphrodisiac powers.

In a 1-quart saucepan, mix all ingredients. Bring to a boil over medium-high heat. Reduce heat and simmer for 5 minutes.

Serve hot to someone you love who needs a kiss to make it better.

Green Mango Salad

xxxxxx

Serves 4–6

1 tablespoon fish sauce

1/4 cup lime juice

1 Thai chile, thinly sliced

1 tablespoon honey

Dash of toasted sesame oil

4 green mangos,
peeled and grated

1/2 cup Sweet 100
tomatoes, halved

Salt and pepper

Napa cabbage leaves

1/4 cup chopped
roasted peanuts, for garnish

1/4 cup chopped
cilantro leaves, for garnish

Mango is a sexy food. Served in this simple salad, it plays a starring role in a parade of textures and tastes.

To make the dressing, combine the fish sauce, lime juice, chile, honey, and sesame oil, and allow to sit for 10 minutes.

In a non-reactive bowl, combine the mangos, tomatoes, and dressing. Toss well; season to taste with salt and pepper. Allow the mixture to sit for 10 minutes before serving.

Serve on a leaf of Napa cabbage, garnished with chopped peanuts and cilantro.

Chile-Garlic Paste

xxxxxx

This is a recipe for the fresh version of Sriracha, *a popular Thai condiment that is available in Asian markets and some regional grocery stores. Once you begin to experiment with its potent flavor combination, we think you'll find it an indispensable condiment. This paste can be used as you would any hot sauce, to add heat to soups, chilis, noodle dishes, or roast meats and fish.*

With a mortar and pestle or in a food processor, grind the chiles, garlic, and salt to a paste. Add the lime juice. Store in the refrigerator in a jar with a tight-fitting lid.

Makes ½ cup

2 Thai chiles, chopped

2 New Mexico red chiles, chopped

2 cloves garlic, chopped

$1/4$ teaspoon salt

2 tablespoons lime juice

Chile-Ginger Dipping Sauce

xxxxxx

Chile with ginger is a classic Asian combination. Considering all the ailments said to be cured by one or the other in ancient tradition, we figure this dish can cure anything.

Combine all ingredients, stirring until the sugar dissolves; allow to sit for 10–15 minutes before serving. The dipping sauce can be prepared up to 1 day in advance but is best when fresh.

Makes 1 cup

2 Thai chiles, sliced thin

2-inch piece of ginger, peeled and chopped fine

2 tablespoons sugar

$1/4$ cup fish sauce

$1/4$ cup lime juice

$1/4$ cup water

Oysters with Asian-inspired Mignonette

xxxxxx

Serves 2–4

2 teaspoons finely
diced shallots

1/2 teaspoon fresh ground
black pepper

1/2 Thai chile, seeds and ribs
removed, sliced very thin

1/4 cup rice vinegar

1/4 teaspoon soy sauce

1/4 teaspoon toasted
sesame oil

12 fresh oysters,
shucked, in their shells

4 cups crushed ice

Oysters may not be indigenous to the desert, but they are con-sidered a wonderful complement to spice in Asian cuisines. They are also among the most seductive foods on the planet. This dish brings a one–two punch that absolutely cannot be beat.

Mix shallot, pepper, and chile slices in a small glass or ceramic bowl. Stir in the vinegar, soy sauce, and sesame oil. Allow to sit for at least 30 minutes.

To serve: On a platter, arrange the oysters in the crushed ice. Set the dish of prepared "mignonette" sauce in the center, with a small spoon.

Chicken Skewers with Spicy Peanut Dipping Sauce

xxxxxx

Peanuts, extremely popular in Southeast Asian cooking, are among our favorite aphrodisiacs. As a first course or entrée salad, serve larger skewers on a bed of Fennel-Apple Slaw (see page 14) with the dipping sauce drizzled on top or in a small side cup. For hors d'ouevres, place a half melon or half pineapple face-down on a platter, surrounded by rock salt. Cut a hole in the center of the fruit to hold a cup of the dipping sauce; arrange skewers around the cup, with the points stuck into the fruit. Be sure to offer a basket to dispose of the skewers.

To make the sauce, use a food processor fitted with the standard "S" blade. Process the peanut butter, honey, lime juice, vinegar, jalapeño, garlic, ginger, and sesame oil until smooth. If the sauce is too thick, drizzle in water, 1 tablespoon at a time, while the processor is running, until you achieve the desired consistency. Season with salt and pepper. The sauce can be stored in a covered bowl in the refrigerator for 3–5 days. Bring to room temperature and stir well before serving.

In a small bowl, combine 2 tablespoons of the dipping sauce with lime juice and peanut oil. Put chicken strips and marinade into a gallon-size zip-top bag in a bowl in the refrigerator for at least 30 minutes, or up to 2 hours.

Preheat a grill or stovetop grilling pan on high heat. If using bamboo skewers, soak them in water for 5 minutes. Weave the chicken pieces onto metal or bamboo skewers. For first course or entrée-size portions, weave 2 ounces of chicken onto each of

Serves 4

1/2 cup creamy peanut butter

1 tablespoon honey

1 tablespoon lime juice

1 tablespoon rice wine vinegar

1/2 jalapeño chile, cut into pieces (seeds and ribs optional)

1 clove garlic

1-inch piece of fresh ginger, peeled and cut into pieces

1 teaspoon toasted sesame oil

Water as necessary

Salt and pepper

2 tablespoons of the dipping sauce

1 tablespoon lime juice

1 tablespoon peanut oil

1 pound boneless skinless chicken breasts, cut into 1/2-inch-thick strips

Salt and pepper

Oil for grill

8 skewers (2 per person). Decrease amount of chicken and skewer size for hors d'oeuvres portions of ½–1 ounce per skewer.

Lightly oil the grill grates. Lay the skewers on the grill with the ends away from direct heat, if possible. For larger skewers, cook for approximately 4 minutes per side. Smaller skewers could cook in as little as 1 minute per side, depending on thickness and on the grill.

Jalapeño.

Vietnamese Rice Paper Rolls

xxxxxx

4 servings

1 ounce dried rice vermicelli

4 medium-large (fresh or frozen) cooked shrimp, peeled and deveined

1 carrot, peeled and julienned

1/2 red bell pepper, julienned

1 teaspoon rice wine vinegar

Dash of toasted sesame oil

4 rice papers (8-inch size)

8 edible flowers, optional

12–15 fresh mint leaves

1/4 cup fresh cilantro leaves

4 scallion greens, julienned

Chile-Ginger Dipping Sauce (see page 41), for serving

Although the summer roll (which is served cold and uncooked, unlike spring rolls) is unique to Vietnam, its juxtaposition of flavors strives for very much the same effect as Southwestern cuisine, pitting the heat of chiles against a refreshing combination of tartness and freshness (in this case, cooling mint and tangy vinegar). Good flowers to use in this recipe include organic, pesticide-free herb blossoms (such as chives, garlic, rosemary, thyme, or basil), nasturtiums, chrysanthemums, carnations, roses, pansies, violas, or violets.

Soak the rice vermicelli in warm water for 20 minutes, then drain; cook for 2 minutes in boiling salted water, shock with cold water, and drain well. Cut the shrimp in half lengthwise. In separate bowls, dress the carrot and bell pepper strips in the vinegar and sesame oil.

Arrange a work space with a bowl of water, one damp cloth to roll on, and each prepared ingredient in separate bowls. Also, prepare a baking sheet lined with plastic wrap and a second damp cotton towel to cover the finished rolls, so they won't dry out.

Working with one sheet at a time, soak the rice paper in water until it is soft and pliable (up to 30 seconds) and move to the damp towel work surface. If you are including edible flowers in your summer rolls, arrange 2 flowers, face down, in the center of the rice paper (optional); place two shrimp halves end to end on top of the flowers. Arrange several mint leaves, followed by 1/4 each of the cilantro leaves, scallion greens, carrots, bell pepper, and vermicelli along the length of the shrimp, close together. Fold the top and bottom thirds of the rice paper down onto the filling; then carefully roll this rectangle into a compact tube shape (burrito-style), as tightly as possible. Dampen the edge with water to seal. Place seam side down on the baking sheet. Cover with the damp towel, then with more plastic wrap. Repeat with the remaining rice paper sheets. Serve soon after completion, or they can be stored for up to 2 hours in the refrigerator.

Serve with Chile-Ginger Dipping Sauce.

Coconut Curry Steamed Mussels

xxxxxx

Serves 4

1 tablespoon peanut oil

1/2 cup finely diced onion

1 tablespoon
Thai green curry paste

1 jalapeño, seeds and ribs
removed, julienned

1 can (14 ounces)
coconut milk

1-inch piece of ginger,
peeled and finely diced

1-inch piece of lemongrass
(the tender bulb end),
roughly chopped

2 pounds mussels,
well cleaned and
beards removed

Juice of 1 lime

1 teaspoon fish sauce

2 teaspoons honey

Salt and pepper

1/4 cup chopped
cilantro leaves,
for garnish

Coconuts are one of the most sensory-stimulating ingredients shared by Eastern and Southwestern cooking.

In a stockpot, heat the peanut oil over medium-high heat. Add the onion and sauté until tender. Add the curry paste and jalapeño, sautéing for an additional 2 minutes. Add the coconut milk, ginger, and lemongrass; bring to a simmer.

Add the mussels to the pot, then cover and simmer over medium heat until the mussels all open. Remove the mussels to a serving bowl. Discard any mussels that have not opened. Add the lime juice, fish sauce, and honey to the pot. Bring to a boil. Season with salt and pepper to taste.

Pour the liquid over the mussels and garnish with chopped cilantro.

Thai Firecracker Rice

XXXXXX

Serves 4–6

2 cups chicken or vegetable stock

1 cup long-grain rice

1/2 teaspoon salt

1 tablespoon peanut oil

1 teaspoon red curry paste

1/2 cup coconut milk

1/2 cup frozen peas, thawed

1/2 cup diced carrots

1 Anaheim chile, roasted, peeled, and diced

1/4 cup diced red bell pepper

1/2 teaspoon Thai fish sauce

1 teaspoon soy sauce

1/4 cup chopped roasted peanuts, for garnish

2 tablespoons chopped cilantro leaves, for garnish

1/2 cup bean sprouts, for garnish

4–6 lime wedges, for garnish

In Thailand, the traditional purpose of fried rice is to use up the previous day's leftovers. Feel free to toss in any favorite vegetables lingering in your fridge. This dish makes a wonderful accompaniment to Chilled Grilled Shrimp (see page 15).

To prepare the rice, bring the stock to a boil in a medium saucepan with a tight-fitting lid. Add the rice and salt; return to a boil. Reduce heat to low and allow the rice to simmer, covered, for 20 minutes. Remove from heat and allow to stand for 5 minutes, then fluff with a fork.

Heat a wok or large sauté pan over high heat. Heat the peanut oil; add the curry paste and stir well for 1 minute. Add the coconut milk and stir until combined. Add the peas, carrots, chile, bell pepper, fish sauce, and soy sauce. Season with additional soy sauce to taste; simmer until the carrots are tender.

Fold in the cooked rice and heat through. Serve hot, garnished with chopped peanuts, cilantro, bean sprouts, and a lime wedge.

Cubanelle peppers.

A Saucy Italian

xxxxxx

*Makes approximately
1 cup*

2 Roma tomatoes,
seeded and diced

1/2 teaspoon salt

6 basil leaves

1 tablespoon
extra-virgin olive oil

1 clove garlic, finely diced

1 teaspoon red wine vinegar

1 teaspoon red chile flakes

Additional salt and pepper

This makes a great topping for bruschetta (grilled bread rubbed with garlic), a salsa for grilled steak or chicken, or a cool sauce for hot pasta. As a matter of fact, Annette has found a use for it on just about everything—even her breakfast eggs!

Toss the diced tomatoes with the salt and allow to sit for 2–3 minutes until some of the juices are released.

Chiffonade the basil as follows: Stack the basil leaves and roll tightly like a cigar. With a sharp knife, cut the "cigar" into very thin slices. These slices will unroll into thin ribbons of basil.

Add the olive oil, garlic, vinegar, chile flakes, and basil to the tomatoes. Season with additional salt and freshly ground black pepper, to taste.

Refrigerate for at least 1 hour before using, up to 3 days.

Grape Salsa

xxxxxx

For this variation on a Southwestern classic, using grapes instead of tomatoes gives a refreshing sweetness that is the perfect partner for baked Brie cheese served on toasted baguette slices—a very sexy combination.

Assemble all ingredients. Mix the grapes, chile, pepper, lime juice, and honey. Add the cilantro. Season with salt to taste. Allow to sit for 1 hour before serving.

Makes approximately 1 cup

1 cup seedless Red Flame grapes, diced

$1/2$ serrano chile, seeds and ribs removed, diced

2 tablespoons finely diced red bell pepper

2 tablespoons lime juice

1 teaspoon honey

2 tablespoons chopped cilantro leaves

Salt

Piquant Pepper Pesto

xxxxxx

This Southwestern variation on an Italian-American classic teases the senses with a hint of heat. It's perfect for pasta, but if you're like Amy, you'll find yourself eating it straight from the spoon.

Roast the peppers and chiles over open flames until all skin is charred. Allow to cool in a bag or covered bowl. Peel away all charred skin; remove seeds and ribs.

In a food processor fitted with a standard "S" blade, combine the roasted peppers and chiles, piñon nuts, basil, cheese, and garlic. Pulse until a paste is formed. Drizzle in the olive oil and lemon juice with the blade running. Do not over-process. Season to taste with salt and pepper.

Makes approximately 2 cups

4 red bell peppers (or the equivalent in jarred roasted red peppers)

2 poblano chiles

1 New Mexico red chile

$1/2$ cup toasted piñon nuts (or try pepitas—toasted pumpkin seeds)

$1/2$ cup basil leaves

$1/4$ cup grated Parmesan cheese

3 cloves garlic

$1/2$ cup olive oil

1 teaspoon lemon juice

Salt and pepper

Chipotle Hummus

xxxxxx

Makes approximately 2 cups

1 chipotle chile, canned in adobo sauce

2 cloves garlic

1 can (14 ounces) garbanzo beans, drained and rinsed

1/2 teaspoon ground cumin

1/2 teaspoon ground coriander

1/2 cup tahini (toasted sesame paste)

3 tablespoons fresh lemon juice

2 tablespoons olive oil

2 tablespoons water, as necessary

2 tablespoons chopped cilantro leaves

Salt and pepper

Southwest meets Middle East in a creamy, tongue-tingling duo. A perfect dip for a sophisticated cocktail spread, this can also be the catalyst for a romantic evening for two.

In a food processor fitted with the standard "S" blade, chop 1 chipotle chile from a can of *chipotle en adobo* with 2 cloves of garlic. Add the garbanzo beans, cumin, coriander, tahini, and lemon juice. Puree, drizzling the olive oil in while the processor is running.

Taste the hummus. Blend in a little of the water, as necessary, to thin the mixture to your desired consistency; fold in the cilantro. Season with salt and pepper, to taste.

Scrape into a bowl, cover with plastic wrap (touching the surface), refrigerate for at least 1 hour, up to 3 days. Serve as a dip for pita chips, tortilla chips, or crostini. This can also be spread on seasoned fish fillets that have been brushed with olive oil, then baked in a 350-degree F oven for approximately 15 minutes. Drizzle with lemon juice before serving.

Spicy Onion Harissa

xxxxxx

An exotic departure from American uses for chile heat, this recipe represents the Eastern tradition for sexy spice at its finest.

Makes approximately 1 cup

Combine the tomato paste with the coriander, dry and fresh chiles, and bell pepper. Slowly whisk in the oil and vinegar. Add the scallions, red onion, and garlic. Stir well, seasoning with salt and pepper.

Let stand at room temperature for at least 1 hour, up to 8 hours. Stir well before serving.

2 tablespoons tomato paste

$1/2$ teaspoon ground coriander

1 teaspoon red chile flakes

1 small Thai chile, seeds and ribs carefully removed, thinly sliced

$1/4$ red bell pepper, finely diced

$1/2$ cup olive oil

$1/4$ cup red wine vinegar

2 scallions, thinly sliced (white and light green parts only)

$1/2$ cup thinly sliced red onion

1 clove garlic, minced

Salt and pepper

Tzatziki

xxxxx

Makes approximately 1½ cups

8 ounces plain yogurt (don't use non-fat or low-fat)

1 cucumber, peeled and grated (avoid including the seeds)

1 teaspoon salt

½ New Mexico green chile, seeds and ribs removed, finely diced

½ New Mexico red chile, seeds and ribs removed, finely diced

2 cloves garlic, crushed

½ teaspoon ground coriander

Zest of 1 lemon

1 tablespoon lemon juice

2 tablespoons chopped fresh chives

Salt and pepper

We've made over Greece's famous yogurt dip, giving it a lift with some Southwestern heat. This is a wonderful dip for fresh veggies, pita chips, and fingers. The secret to a rich, satisfying tzatziki is draining the yogurt overnight to an almost-cream-cheese consistency.

The day before preparing, set a small strainer lined with a coffee filter over a bowl; pour the yogurt into the filter. Allow to sit, loosely covered, in the refrigerator overnight to drain.

One hour before preparing, peel and grate the cucumber. Toss it with the salt; set the cucumber in a strainer over a bowl in the refrigerator for approximately 1 hour to drain off excess water.

Combine the yogurt, cucumber, green and red chiles, garlic, coriander, lemon zest, lemon juice, and chives in a non-reactive bowl. Season with salt and pepper to taste. Place in a covered bowl in the refrigerator for at least 1 hour before serving, to allow the flavors to meld.

Mango-Ginger Salsa

xxxxxx

Tropical fruit can take salsa to a whole new level. Adding ginger gives this colorful salsa an added aphrodisiac punch.

Assemble all ingredients. Mix the mango, ginger, peppers, lime juice, and honey. Add the cilantro. Season with salt and pepper to taste. Allow to sit for 1 hour before serving.

Serve this salsa as a dip with chips, over grilled chicken or fish, or mixed with mayonnaise as a sandwich spread.

Makes approximately 1 cup

1 mango, peeled and diced into small cubes

1-inch piece fresh ginger, peeled and finely chopped

$1/2$ jalapeño pepper, finely diced

$1/2$ red bell pepper, finely diced

Juice of 1 lime

1 teaspoon honey

$1/4$ cup chopped fresh cilantro

Salt and pepper

Raspberry Glaze

xxxxxx

Use this bright, sweet-hot sauce to glaze fish, chicken, or pork, as well as to add sweet zing to salad dressings. Or, if your taste leans more toward a sweet tooth, brush it on a fruit tart for a sweet-hot glaze.

Cook the frozen raspberries with the vinegar in a non-reactive $1\frac{1}{2}$-quart saucepan over medium heat until the raspberries are broken down.

Add the sugar, jam or jelly, jalapeño, chile powder, and soy sauce. Simmer over low heat, stirring often, for 15 minutes. Strain to remove most of the seeds. Season to taste. The sauce will thicken as it cools.

This glaze can be stored in a tightly covered container in the refrigerator for 1 week or in the freezer for up to 1 month.

Makes 2 cups

1 package (10 ounces) frozen raspberries

$1/4$ cup apple cider vinegar

$1/4$ cup sugar

$1/4$ cup raspberry jam or jelly (with or without seeds)

1 red jalapeño chile, seeds and ribs removed, finely diced

1 teaspoon chipotle chile powder

1 teaspoon soy sauce

Salt and pepper

Red Fresno chiles.

Basic Cocktail Rim

XXXXXX

One thing that makes a simple cocktail special is the sparkle and extra boost of flavor that comes from a creative rim garnish. Add a little spice to your next Bloody Mary, martini, or even a classic fresh-squeezed lemonade. Amy uses this garnish with just about everything. A favorite is on a champagne glass filled with a bubbly Brut and a splash of Alize. A sweet version of this dry mix can be made by swapping in sugar in place of the salt.

Yield amount will vary

2 parts kosher salt (or sea salt—we recommend experimenting with salts of different textures)

1 part chile powder (choose your favorite or grind your own)

This recipe is for proportions of ingredients instead of specific amounts, so you can make as much or as little as you desire. The finished product can be stored for a month or more in an airtight container in a cool, dry place.

Moisture It's important to moisten the rim of the glass before dipping into the dry mixture. The most common method is to run a wedge of lemon or lime around the rim before dipping. You could also use simple syrup or, for an even sexier look and an extra aphrodisiac twist, try honey. (The honey runs down the glass and looks very cool, although it is just a touch messy.)

Limeade

xxxxxx

Makes ½ gallon

1 cup sugar

1 cup water

2 jalapeño peppers, split in half

1 cup fresh lime juice

Ice

Additional water

An American take on the aguas frescas *so popular in Mexican marketplaces, this is a refreshing summer sip with just a hint of a kick.*

In a 1-quart saucepan, combine the sugar and 1 cup of water. Bring the mixture to a boil over medium-high heat. Add the chiles, reduce the heat, and simmer for 5 minutes. Cool thoroughly; strain out the chiles.

In a half-gallon jug or pitcher filled halfway with ice, combine the fresh lime juice with the sugar syrup. Top off with enough water to fill the container. You can adjust the flavor with honey or more lime juice.

Chile Cocoa

xxxxxx

Although the process of making drinking chocolate from the fruit of the cacao tree has much improved since the days of the Aztecs, this chile and chocolate combination comes close to recreating Montezuma's favorite aphrodisiac drink.

Combine 1 teaspoon of sugar with ¼ teaspoon of chile powder on a small plate. Dip the cut side of the marshmallow halves into the mixture. Set aside, chile side up.

In a small saucepan, combine the water, cocoa, tablespoon of sugar, salt, ½ teaspoon of chile powder, and nutmeg. Bring to a boil over medium heat, stirring often, for 2 minutes.

Add vanilla and milk. Heat thoroughly but do not boil.

Remove from heat, whip until frothy, and serve hot. Garnish with chile marshmallows floating chile side up.

Serves 2

1 teaspoon sugar

¼ teaspoon chipotle chile powder

2 large marshmallows, cut in half

¼ cup water

2 tablespoons good-quality unsweetened cocoa

1 tablespoon sugar (more, if desired)

Pinch of salt

½ teaspoon chipotle chile powder

Pinch of nutmeg

½ teaspoon vanilla extract

1 cup milk

Pineapple-Jalapeño–Infused Vodka

xxxxx

Makes approximately 1 quart

1 ripe pineapple, peeled, cored, and cut into cubes

2 jalapeño peppers, cut in half

1 quart good-quality vodka

For this recipe, you will need a half-gallon jar with a tight-fitting lid. To get a full-flavored infusion, please allow 1 to 2 weeks in the refrigerator.

Combine the fruit, chiles, and vodka in a jar with a tight-fitting lid. Refrigerate or store in a cool place out of direct sunlight. Shake the jar every day for the first week and every other day afterward. Allow at least 1 week—ideally 2 weeks—for full infusion.

Serving suggestions Strain the vodka before using; it will be cloudy even after straining. Serve over ice straight or with a splash of club soda. You can also blend this vodka with crushed ice, pineapple juice, and crème de coconut for a sweet piña colada-style treat.

Serrano chiles.

Mexican Chocolate Martini

XXXXXX

Serves 2

This variation on the bartender's flirtiest drink takes Montezuma's aphrodisiac drinking chocolate to a whole new level. Be sure to chill your martini glasses ahead of time.

1 1/2 teaspoons sugar

1/2 teaspoon cocoa

1/4 teaspoon ground cinnamon

1/2 teaspoon red chile powder

add 1/2 c
2 ounces chocolate liqueur

2 ounces chile-infused vodka (directions follow)

2 ounces vanilla vodka

1/2 ounce cinnamon syrup (for example, Torani)

1/2 ounce whipping cream

2 thin cinnamon sticks

Combine the sugar, cocoa, cinnamon, and chile powder for the rim coating and pour evenly onto a small plate. Chill two sexy martini glasses in the freezer. Before preparing the martini, moisten the rims of the glasses with chocolate liqueur and dip them in the sugar mixture, coating the rims evenly.

Pour the vodkas, chocolate liqueur, and cinnamon syrup into a cocktail shaker half filled with cracked ice. Shake vigorously for 1 minute.

Swirl in the whipping cream; strain evenly into 2 martini glasses. Garnish with cinnamon sticks.

Note: To make your own chile-infused vodka, add 2 hot cherry peppers and 2 serrano chiles, with their stems removed, to a liter bottle of vodka. Allow to sit for 2 days before using.

Three Sisters' Bloody Marys

xxxxxx

This recipe is a standard Sunday must-have in the Tomei household when Annette and her sisters gather for good gossip.

In a blender or food processor, puree the tomatoes, chiles, and scallions. Strain well and season with salt and pepper. Reserve. Stir well before using.

In a large pitcher, combine the horseradish, Worcestershire sauce, lemon or lime juice, and vodka. Add 1 quart of the prepared tomato juice (use spicy V8 juice if fresh is not available). Stir well; season to taste with hot sauce, celery salt, and pepper.

Fill 4 tall glasses with ice, pour the Bloody Mary mixture over the ice, and garnish with the skewered olives.

Serves 4

4 pounds heirloom tomatoes (or other garden-fresh tomatoes), cut into chunks

2 fresh chiles, cut into pieces

4 scallions, cut into pieces

Salt and pepper

2 tablespoons grated horseradish

$1/_2$ teaspoon Worcestershire sauce

2 tablespoons fresh lime or lemon juice

4 ounces premium vodka (chile-infused vodka, if desired)

Hot sauce

Celery salt

Freshly ground black pepper

Ice

8 blue cheese-stuffed olives, 2 each on 4 skewers

Habañero chiles.

Chile-Spiced Grilled Fruit

xxxxxx

The heat of chiles adds an enticing taste sensation to the smoky sweetness of grilled ripe fruit. This recipe makes a great way to end a meal prepared on the grill. Try grilled fruit over ice cream or sorbet, with biscotti, or on a graham cracker with toasted marshmallows.

If your grill is not already hot from preparing the main course, heat it to medium-low. If the grates are dirty from use, clean them or cover them with aluminum foil.

Combine the oil, juice, and chopped chile; scrape the vanilla bean into the mixture, then include the pod. Allow to sit for 10 minutes. Combine the salt, chile powder, and sugar; reserve.

Set the fruit on a baking pan or large plate. Brush generously with the marinade mixture on all sides. Allow to sit for 5 minutes. Also brush the grill grates or aluminum foil with some of the marinade.

If grilling directly on the grates, brush off some of the marinade to prevent flare-ups. Season your fruit pieces with the salt mixture. Gently place the fruit, cut side down, on the grill. Do not move it for at least 2 minutes. Cooking time will depend on the texture of the fruit. Turn it over when dark golden grill marks are visible. Use a spatula to gently remove the fruit from the grill.

Serves 4

1/4 cup canola oil

1 tablespoon citrus juice

1 serrano chile, chopped (with seeds and ribs)

1/4 vanilla bean pod

1 teaspoon salt

1/4 teaspoon chile powder

1 teaspoon sugar

4 serving-size pieces of fresh, ripe fruits (for example, 2 large peaches, cut in half; 4 slices of pineapple, 1-inch thick; 4 bananas, peeled and cut in half lengthwise; or 2 pears, halved and cored)

"Secret Passion" Crème Brûlée

xxxxx

Serves 4

1 cup heavy cream

1/2 vanilla bean pod, split

1 dry habañero chile, split in half

6 egg yolks

1/3 cup sugar

1 tablespoon dark rum

Approximately 1/2 cup sugar for topping

We like to think our hot twist on this sinfully creamy classic has a sweet secret sure to heat things up!

Preheat oven to 325 degrees F. Have the following items ready before you begin: a large bowl of ice with a small amount of water, a medium-size bowl that fits into the ice bath, a whisk, a ladle, a wooden spoon, a fine strainer, and a second medium-size mixing bowl. You will also need 4 custard baking cups (¾-cup ramekins or crème brûlée dishes) set in a baking pan with sides.

Pour the cream into a 1½-quart saucepan. Scrape the contents of the vanilla bean pod into the cream, then add the pod and the habañero chile. Bring to a fast simmer over medium-high heat. Be careful not to let it boil over.

While the cream is heating, beat the egg yolks in a medium-size mixing bowl. Add the ⅓ cup of sugar in a steady stream, whisking constantly. Do not allow the mixture to clump on the sides of the bowl.

When the cream boils, remove it from the heat; temper the egg yolk mixture by ladling in some of hot liquid, whisking constantly. Add the tempered egg yolk mixture to the hot cream, stirring the custard until it is well combined. Stir in the rum.

Place the unused medium-size mixing bowl over the ice bath. Strain the custard into the bowl, stirring often to cool the mixture evenly and quickly. Fill the custard cups three-quarters full. Move to the center oven rack, then fill the baking pan with very hot tap water to halfway up the sides of the custard cups, then top off the custard cups with the remaining custard. Bake for 30 minutes or until custard sets up (a firm jiggle when the side of the custard cup is tapped). Remove the custard cups from the baking pan while it is still on the oven rack, being careful not to get water into any of the custards. Cool completely. This can be done up to 2 days in advance. Keep the custards wrapped individually in the refrigerator.

Before serving, heat the broiler portion of the oven. Sprinkle a tablespoon (or more) of sugar over the surface of each cool custard, tapping to cover evenly and to remove any excess. Place the custards on a sheet pan in the broiler with the door open for approximately 2 minutes; turn as necessary to brown the sugar crust evenly. Be careful not to overcook. Allow the crust to set for 5–10 minutes before serving on a dessert plate with a crisp cookie or fresh berries.

Note: You may also use a special propane torch (available in gourmet kitchen supply stores) to caramelize the sugar crust. Follow the manufacturer's safety instructions for an even crust.

Orange Chipotle Truffles

xxxxxx

Makes approximately 24 truffles

1 cup heavy cream

1 tablespoon sugar

1 tablespoon butter

1 teaspoon finely grated orange zest

1 teaspoon chipotle chile powder

8 ounces semisweet or bittersweet chocolate, chopped evenly

1 tablespoon orange liqueur

1/4 teaspoon salt

1/4 teaspoon vanilla extract

1/4 cup cocoa

2 tablespoons powdered sugar

1 teaspoon chipotle chile powder

Chocolate with chile is a Central American aphrodisiac combination dating back further than recorded time. We've added orange to augment both the bite of bitter chocolate and the chile's sweet sting.

Heat the cream, sugar, butter, orange zest, and 1 teaspoon of chile powder to a boil over medium-high heat. Be careful not to boil over. Remove from the heat and stir in the chocolate, liqueur, salt, and vanilla, until smooth.

Pour into an 8-inch baking pan, cover loosely, and refrigerate until firm.

Combine the cocoa, powdered sugar, and additional teaspoon of chile powder in a shallow bowl. In batches, scoop out teaspoon- or tablespoon-size portions of the truffle mixture; roll them into balls and coat them with the cocoa mixture. Set the balls on a baking sheet and refrigerate until firm. Store in an airtight container with the cocoa mixture in the refrigerator for up to 1 week, or freeze.

Mexican Chocolate Torte

xxxxxx

Makes a 9-inch cake (serves 12–16)

1 1/2 cups graham cracker crumbs

1/2 cup cocoa

1/2 cup sugar

5 tablespoons butter, melted

1/2 teaspoon ground cinnamon

1/2 teaspoon hot New Mexico chile powder

1 teaspoon salt

Cooking spray

12 ounces semi-sweet chocolate chips

3 eggs

1/4 cup sugar

1 teaspoon vanilla

1/2 teaspoon ground cinnamon

1/2 teaspoon hot New Mexico chile powder

1/2 teaspoon salt

1 cup heavy cream

Chocolate has been a treasured ingredient in Mexican tradition since the days of the Aztecs' supreme reign. Use a premium chocolate in combination with "real" cinnamon (not the poor cousin sold in most grocery spice sections) for a taste experience that would have made Montezuma sigh in satisfaction.

For the crust, blend together the graham cracker crumbs, cocoa, 1/2 cup of sugar, butter, 1/2 teaspoon of ground cinnamon, 1/2 teaspoon of chile powder, and teaspoon of salt. Press firmly into the bottom of a 9-inch springform pan that has been sprayed lightly with cooking spray.

For the filling, place the chocolate chips, eggs, 1/4 cup of sugar, vanilla, additional 1/2 teaspoon of ground cinnamon, additional 1/2 teaspoon of chile powder, and 1/2 teaspoon of salt in a blender. Heat the cream to a rapid simmer, then pour it into the chocolate mixture with the blender running. Blend until smooth.

Pour the filling into the crust. Refrigerate or freeze for at least 4 hours. Can be frozen for up to 1 month.

Allow to sit at room temperature for 30 minutes before serving. Serve with whipped cream and fresh berries.

Red Hot Strawberry Shortcake

xxxxxx

For this adult version of an American classic dessert, use your favorite shortcake recipe or a fresh angel food cake purchased from the bakery at your local grocery store.

Chill a steep-sided bowl for the whipped cream. Before preparing the caramel sauce for the strawberries, have all your ingredients assembled, along with a small pastry brush in a cup of cool water. You may also wish to have long rubber gloves on when you finish the caramel sauce, since it tends to splash.

In a heavy 1-quart saucepan, combine the sugar and 1 tablespoon of the water. Brush the inside of the pan with the wet pastry brush to make sure there is no sugar stuck to the sides. Over medium-high heat, bring the sugar mixture to a boil. Do not stir; gently swirl the liquid after all the sugar has melted. Reduce the heat and swirl occasionally as the sugar begins to caramelize. When the caramel is deep golden in color, remove from the heat (put the gloves on if you like) and very carefully pour the ¼ cup water down the inside of the pot into the caramel. It will sputter and splash a bit for a few seconds—be careful not to allow it to get on your skin. Swirl to re-melt the sugar into the water. Add the chile, then scrape the vanilla bean into the caramel, discarding the pod. Stir to combine. If necessary, place the pot over low heat to re-melt the sugar. Cool before continuing. If necessary, add more water to thin to a thick syrup consistency.

Serves 4

½ cup sugar

¼ cup plus
1 tablespoon water

½ red serrano chile,
seeds and ribs
removed, sliced thin

½ vanilla bean pod, split

1 pint strawberries,
cleaned, hulled, and sliced

Pinch of salt

½ cup whipping cream

1 tablespoon
powdered sugar

¼ teaspoon red
chile powder

Place the strawberries in a medium-size mixing bowl. Pour the chile-caramel mixture over the top, season with a pinch of salt, and fold together gently. Chill.

In the chilled steep-sided bowl, whisk the cream rapidly until it begins to thicken. Add the powdered sugar and chile powder, whisking until stiff peaks form. Be careful not to over-beat the cream.

Place a shortcake or slice of angel food cake in each of 4 shallow bowls or dessert dishes. Ladle approximately ½ cup of the strawberry mixture over the top and garnish with a dollop of spiced whipped cream.

Scoville—The Chile Heat Meter

APPENDIX I.

The Scoville test is the standard for measuring chile pungency. The scale is an approximation, since chile heat can vary from pepper to pepper. (And, as a matter of fact, soil and climate variations can give two chiles of the same variety vastly differing tastes.) Drying a chile is believed to increase heat by approximately 10 times.

NAME	SCOVILLE UNITS
Bell pepper	0
Anaheim, New Mexico	500–1,000
Poblano	1,000–2,000
Ancho	1,000–2500
Pasilla	1,000–2,500
Jalapeño	2,500–5,000
Serrano	5,000–6,000
Chipotle	5,000–10,000
Chile de árbol	15,000–20,000
Cayenne	30,000–40,000
Thai	60,000–80,000
Red habañero	150,000
Orange habañero	200,000–250,000
Pure capsaicin	16,000,000

Tips for Handling and Preparation

APPENDIX II.

Chiles are hot not only to the tongue but to the touch. When handling varieties with a lot of heat, be sure to wear rubber gloves and make sure not to touch your eyes, nose, or lips.

Most of the chile's capsaicin, the ingredient with all the heat, is in the fruit's white interior veins and seed pods. To reduce the amount of heat the pepper brings to a dish, carefully remove the veins, pods, and seeds and dispose before you remove your gloves. Be sure to thoroughly clean your cutting board after cutting chiles.

For recipes in which you want to keep the chile whole, roll the whole fruit between your thumb and fingers before removing the stem, then shake out the seeds and wash the chile inside and out.

Fresh chiles can be stored whole in the refrigerator for several weeks. Once cut, they will last 2–3 days.

High-quality dried chiles can be kept for as long as two years. They are best preserved in an airtight container in a dark place. Direct sunlight will cause their color to fade.

Great Wines for Chile Lovers

APPENDIX III. We are both of the opinion that choosing a wine you enjoy is far more important than choosing a wine you think will match your meal. But serving wines with chiles can be tricky. The bite of the chile can throw off flavor perception of the wine, making a favorite wine suddenly taste unpleasant.

We've included suggestions of a few wines we have enjoyed with spicy, chile-based dishes, but we recommend that you just use this as a guide for styles with which to experiment. We're sure you'll soon be composing your own list of favorite chile-friendly wines.

White & Sparkling Freixenet Carta Nevada Brut Cava, Dr. Konstantin Frank Johannisberg Semi-Dry Riesling, Craggy Range Sauvignon Blanc, Hugel Riesling, Brundlmayer Ried Lamm Gruner Veltliner

Red Grant Burge Holy Trinity, Pedroncelli Pedroni-Bushnell Vineyard Dry Creek Valley Zinfandel, Osborne Solaz Red Table Wine

Dessert Dashe Cellars Late Harvest Zinfandel, Inniskillin Vidal Ice Wine

Additional Resources

Fiery Foods Website, www.fiery-foods.com (extensive resource website for chiles and barbecue)

Chile Pepper magazine, 800-937-8963, www.chilepepper-.com (the only magazine solely dedicated to chile peppers)

Chile Pepper Institute at New Mexico University, www.chile-pepperinstitute.org (the world's largest research center for chiles)

Chile Appreciation Society International, www.chili.org (creators of the International Chili Cookoff)

APPENDIX IV.

INDEX